Leo and Luna's Lockbox

BRIDGETTE CASKEY

Leo and Luna's Lockbox
Copyright © 2021 by Bridgette Caskey

All rights reserved. No part of this book may be photocopied, reproduced, distributed, uploaded, or transmitted in any form or by any means, or stored in a database or retrieval system, without the prior written permission of the publisher.

J. Kenkade Publishing
6104 Forbing Rd
Little Rock, AR 72209
www.jkenkadepublishing.com
Facebook.com/jkenkadepublishing

J. Kenkade Publishing is a registered trademark.

Printed in the United States of America
ISBN 978-1-955186-19-3

This is a work of fiction. Names, characters, businesses, places, events and incidents are either the products of the author's imagination or used in a fictitious manner. Any resemblance to actual persons, living or dead, or actual events is purely coincidental.

Dedicated to:

"Leo! You get out here this second!" yelled Leo's mom.
"You have until the count of three or else!" screamed his dad.
Leo grabbed his backpack and headed out of his den.
He feared that if he didn't come quickly, he would be punished.

I'm doing my very best, thought Leo.

Leo was a very timid cub who always tried to please everyone,
but he especially tried to please his parents.
He loved his mom and dad but really loved going to school too.
Sometimes he didn't even want to go home at the end of the day.
At home he was cold, alone, and scared most of the time.
He would often hear his parents yelling at each other,
and it scared him.

I'm doing my very best, thought Leo.

One morning Leo was awakened by a storm.
He got up out of his bed and got ready for school.
Leo was determined that it would be a good day.
He dreaded going to school some days because he knew
he wouldn't be able to focus on his teacher or learn much that day.
He wished he could go to school and be able to leave all his
worries at home, just forgetting about it all.

I'm doing my very best, thought Leo.

Leo thought and thought of ways he could make that happen. He would often dream of ways that would help him in the classroom—but nothing he dreamed of and tried ever seemed to work.

I'm doing my very best, thought Leo.

One morning was quite different than the rest.
Both his mom and dad seemed to be in very good moods.
Leo got on the bus as usual, and his bus driver,
Mrs. Stephens, noticed Leo was a bit sad.
She told Leo that sometimes when
she was sad or worried about something,
she would write down what was bothering her,
and that would take the worries away.

I'm doing my very best, thought Leo.

When he arrived at school and walked into his classroom, he noticed Luna, another student in his class, slumped down in her chair. Her long ears covered her face and she was crying. Leo wanted so badly to ask what was wrong, but he didn't make it to her desk before the tardy bell rang.

I'm doing my very best, thought Leo.

That day at recess Leo noticed Luna sitting on the
basketball court. She was crying again. This time Leo had
plenty of time to go check on her. He wanted to ask Luna
if there was something he could do to cheer her up.
When he walked up to her, he asked if she were all right.
She replied,
"My grandma is very sick and my mom told me
she wouldn't be with us much longer."
Leo now wished there were a way to take
both of their worries away instead of just his.

I'm doing my very best, thought Leo.

Right before the bell rang to go back inside,
Leo and Luna decided they would meet each day
on the basketball court during their recess time and
share their thoughts until they had a solution to help them
with their worries. They both wanted and needed to be
able to focus while at school.

I'm doing my very best, thought Leo.

As the class walked back into their classroom, their teacher,
Mrs. Dale, was standing at the front of the room next to her desk.
She had a very puzzled look on her face as she asked,
"Where did this box come from? Does this belong to anyone?"
The class looked around. No one was saying a word.
Leo and Luna immediately looked at each other and smiled
the biggest smile. Leo had told Luna about Mrs. Stephens's idea.
Could they use the box to hold all their worries?
Leo couldn't wait to share his thoughts with Luna.

I'm doing my very best, thought Leo.

They decided to both walk home after school that day and talked the whole way. Could they write their worries down and lock them inside a box—the box Mrs. Dale had discovered on her desk? They talked it over and that's exactly what they decided to do. They would call it their "lockbox." The only problem is, they now had to ask Mrs. Dale for the box.

I'm doing my very best, thought Leo.

The next morning they both arrived early to class. They approached the front of the room to share their idea with Mrs. Dale. Leo started talking first. "W—w—w—well, we thought we could use the box to write all our worries on a piece of paper and place them inside the box." Luna added, "This way when we come to school all our worries are here with us but they're locked tightly away in the lockbox." Mrs. Dale thought this was a brilliant idea and agreed to let the entire class participate too. When class started, Mrs. Dale handed out a piece of paper to each student. What will I write? Leo wondered.

I'm doing my very best, thought Leo.

Once everyone was finished and had written all their worries on their pieces of paper, Mrs. Dale opened the box, and one by one, each student dropped his or her worries into the box. When the last one was in, she glued and sealed it tightly with the biggest paper lock so they would know if the box had been tampered with. No one was allowed to look inside or read the worries, not even Mrs. Dale. Leo and Luna felt instant relief and could now focus on their schoolwork so they could learn and become smarter.

I'm doing my very best, thought Leo.

Year after year, Leo and Luna would share their lockbox idea
with their teachers, and each teacher
used a box for this purpose. On the last day of school each year
the teacher would take the box outside and toss it into the
big Dumpster, never to be seen again.
All the students were able to do their very best while at school,
thanks to that special, very secure lockbox.

I've done my very best, thought Leo.

If you suspect a child is being abused or neglected contact your local child protective agency or the Childhelp National Child Abuse Hotline at 1-800-4-A-CHILD (1-800-422-4453)

For free and reasonably priced activities and pintables for this book please visit the author's store at teacherspayteachers.com

About the Author

BRIDGETTE CASKEY is an educator in the central Arkansas area. She is married to her wonderful husband, Jeff. He is retired military and owns a business called AnalytIQ. Together they have 5 beautiful children that range in age from 21 to 9 years old. Bridgette adopted a child from the foster care system. Children's safety and education have been her focus for many years. Bridgette is a huge advocate for teachers being educated in early signs of abuse or neglect. This is why she decided to write a book to aid teachers and counselors across the board in education to help decipher children's struggles. In her spare time, she likes to craft, go camping, fishing, mudding/

ATV riding, watch baseball and is learning to crochet. She also has a successful photography business in the central Arkansas area. In the future it is her hope that this book will save a child's life, if not many children's lives.

Publish Your Book With Us

Our All-Inclusive Self-Publishing Packages
100% Royalties
Professional Proofreading & Editing
Interior Design & Cover Design
Self-Publishing Tutorial & More

For Manuscript Submission or other inquiries:
www.jkenkadepublishing.com
(501) 482-JKEN

Our Motto
"Transforming Life Stories"

Enjoyed this Book?

Check out these children's books by J. Kenkade Publishing

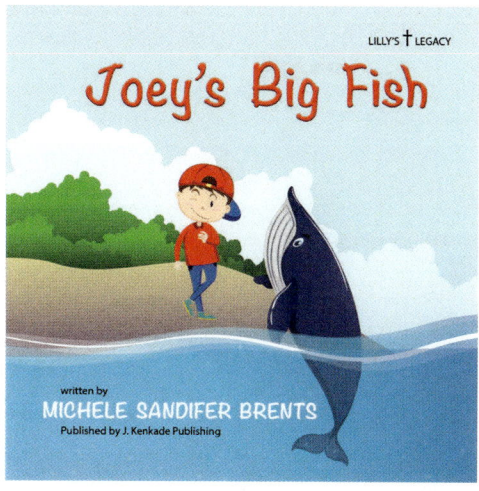

Made in the USA
Coppell, TX
05 February 2022